Torchon Lace Pat

Torchon Lace Patterns

40 patterns with tear-out prickings

Henk Hardeman

B.T. Batsford Ltd, London

The patterns were worked by the following people:

Dana Blokland: 14, 20, 29, 30, 31, 35, 36 and 40.
Sonja Madderom: 17, 18 and 33.
Ria Blanes: 26 and 28.
Mrs. Cohen: 1, 2, 3, 34 and 37.
Mrs. v.d. Zouw: 5, 21, 22 and 33.
Mrs. Hesseling: 4 and 8.
Mrs. Raben: 9 and 19.
Rob Ciermans: 12, 13, 15, 16, 25, 27 and 32.
Henk Hardeman: 4, 6, 7, 10, 11, 23, 24, 38 and 39.

Frontispiece:
Mat worked after an old Dalerna pattern by Henk
Hardeman. The pattern is not yet available.

© Cantecleer bv, de Bilt 1984
First published in Holland, 1984
First published in Great Britain, 1986
© 1986 by B.T. Batsford Ltd.

ISBN 0 7134 4878 4

Printed in Belgium
for the publishers
B.T. Batsford Ltd.
4 Fitzhardinge Street
London W1H 0AH

Photography: Rob Cieremans, Utrecht
Illustrations: Henk Hardeman

In this book you will find both patterns and working diagrams, the latter indicating how the patterns should be worked.

These diagrams are built up with symbols, each symbol representing a stitch.

Although the ground in which the lace is worked is also indicated on the pricking, it is not possible to tell from the prickings which stitches should be used. They are only meant to prevent errors.

Below you will find the explanation of the symbols of both prickings and diagrams.

In practice there are two alternative methods of working, however in the working diagrams and the final result it is not of course obvious which of the two has been used. The explanation of the symbols is in accordance with the method, which leaves the pairs untwisted after the stitch.

Particular Points

Materials

The materials used are given with each diagram, to mention them all here would become too complicated as different materials have been used for each pattern.

Half stitch

A motif with a half stitch filling is often marked in the pricking by a cross, as Fig. 1 shows. In the diagram the half stitches are drawn as in Fig. 2, the passive pairs being represented by a dotted line. Fig. 3 shows the course of the threads of the half stitch.

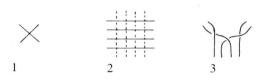

Whole stitch

A section with a whole stitch filling is often marked in the pricking by two slanting lines, as is shown in Fig. 4. In the diagram the whole stitches are drawn as is shown in Fig. 5. Each crossing of lines is a whole stitch. Fig. 6 shows the course of the threads of the whole stitch.

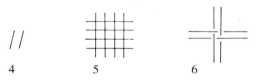

Whole stitch and twist

A whole stitch and twist motif is often marked in the pricking by a double cross as in Fig. 7. In the diagram, whole stitch and twist is drawn as in Fig. 8. The course of the threads of whole stitch and twist is shown as in Fig. 9. In this book only the worker pair is drawn in the prickings, and the diagram indicates where the motif should be worked.

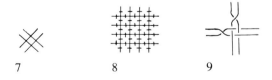

Footside stitch

Fig. 10 is the symbol for the footside stitch and Fig. 11 shows the course of the threads.

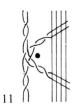

Torchon stitch

Fig. 12 is the symbol for the Torchon stitch and Fig. 13 shows the course of the threads.

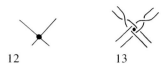

Dieppe stitch

Fig. 14 is the symbol for the Dieppe stitch and Fig. 15 shows the course of the threads. Fig. 16 is the symbol for the Dieppe stitch adjacent to the footside and Fig. 17 shows the course of the threads. The pair leaving and re-entering the footside is only twisted once.

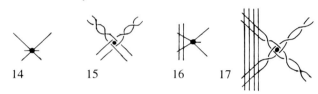

Honeycomb stitch

Fig. 18 is the symbol for the Honeycomb stitch and Fig. 19 shows the course of the threads. Fig. 20 is the symbol for the Honeycomb stitch adjacent to the footside and Fig. 21 shows the course of the threads. The pair leaving and re-entering the footside is only twisted once, and next to the pin, facing the footside, the left-hand pair is also twisted only once between the crossings, see Fig. 21.
If this stitch is adjacent to a right-hand footside, work in reverse.

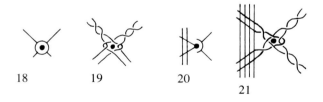

Torchon double stitch

Fig. 22 is the symbol for the Torchon double ground stitch and Fig. 23 shows the course of the threads.

Torchon ground in Torchon stitch

This is shown in Fig. 24; Fig. 25 shows the course of the threads.

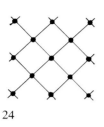

24

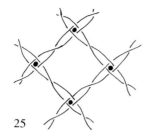

25

Torchon ground in Dieppe stitch

This is shown in Fig. 26; Fig. 27 shows the course of the threads.

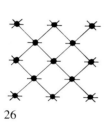

26

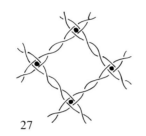

27

Torchon ground in Honeycomb stitch

This is shown in Fig. 28; Fig. 29 shows the course of the threads.

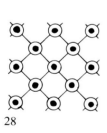

28

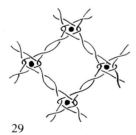

29

Torchon ground in Torchon double stitch

This is shown in Fig. 30; Fig. 31 shows the course of the threads.

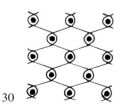

30

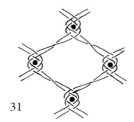

31

Honeycomb net

This is shown in Fig. 32; Fig. 33 shows the course of the threads. The vertical pairs get an extra twist in this net, see Fig. 33. Both Figs. have been drawn in Dieppe stitch, but this net may also be worked in any other stitch.

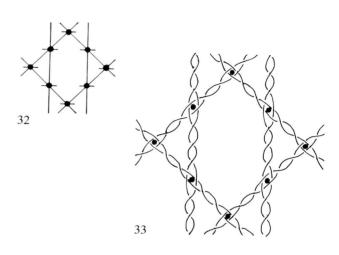

32

33

Diagonal Honeycomb net

This net may be worked in two directions, as Figs. 34 and 35 illustrate. The dotted lines indicate the order of working. Here the diagonal pairs get an extra twist, and again this net may be worked in any other stitch.

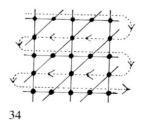

34

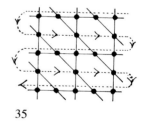

35

Rose ground

This ground is illustrated in the pricking as shown in Fig. 36; work a half stitch between the blocks.
Fig. 37 shows how this ground is illustrated in the pricking, when worked with half stitch, pin, half stitch between the blocks.

36

37

Fig. 38 shows how the Rose ground is illustrated in the pricking when worked in Torchon stitch.
The pinholes 1, 2, 3 and 4 are worked in Torchon stitch in this sequence. Next finish the blocks at 5 and 6 with half stitch, no pin.

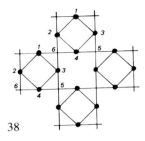

38

Fig. 39 shows the Rose ground when there is a Torchon stitch between the blocks. The sequence of working is similar to the previous Rose ground, but the blocks are finished with half stitch, pin, half stitch.

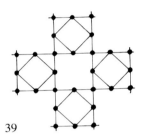

39

Fig. 40 shows a Rose ground with half a honeycomb stitch between the blocks. In the symbol this is illustrated by the omission of the dot, which indicates that only half a honeycomb stitch is worked. Fig. 41 is a Rose ground with a complete honeycomb stitch between the blocks. Finish the blocks with a honeycomb stitch, with pin.

40   41

Bias ground

Figs. 42 and 43 show the Bias ground as illustrated in the pricking. Fig. 44 shows the Bias ground and the sequence of working. Work a Torchon stitch at nos. 1 and 2, no. 3 is a half stitch, nos. 4 and 5 are Torchon stitches again, and at no. 6 work a half stitch once more.
The traversing pairs to the next row *always* get an extra twist to the stitch this gound is worked in.
In this case twice.

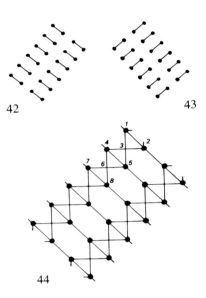

42   43

44

Fig. 45 is a Bias ground worked in honeycomb stitch, but in the opposite direction. The same rule is applied for the traversing pairs: an extra twist to the stitch the ground is worked in, so in this case three times.

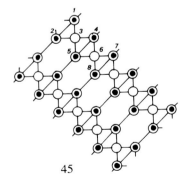

45

Slavonic Rose ground

Fig. 46 shows the pricking for this ground. Fig. 47 gives the sequence of working in Torchon stitch. No. 1 is a Torchon stitch, nos. 2 and 3 are half stitches. No. 4 is a Torchon stitch again, and nos. 5 and 6 are half stitches again. Fig. 48 illustrates this ground worked in Torchon double stitch. Fig. 49 shows the course of the threads of the Slavonic Rose ground when worked in Torchon stitch.

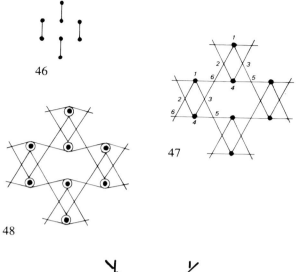

46

47

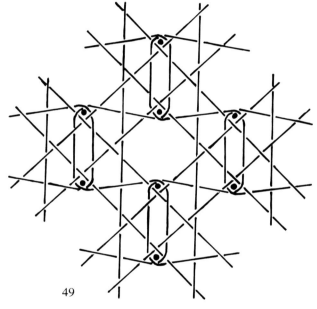

48

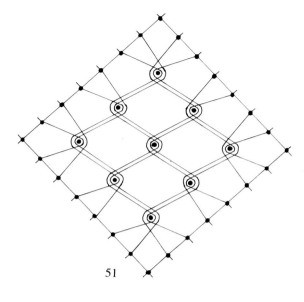

51

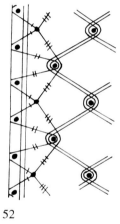

52

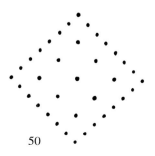

49

Spider ground

Fig. 50 shows the pricking for the Spider ground. Fig. 51 is an illustration of this ground. The pairs to and from the spiders, and between the spiders, are all twisted three times. Fig. 52 shows how the Spider ground is joined to the footside and how many twists are required.

Leaves within a Honeycomb ring

Fig. 53 shows a leaf worked in a honeycomb ring. Note how the beginning and ending of the leaf are worked.

50

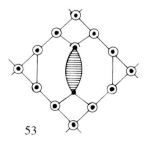

53

Leaves ground

Fig. 54 shows the pricking for the Leaves ground. Fig. 55 is an illustration of this ground. Fig. 56 shows the course of the threads of this ground. The pairs entering the ground are always twisted three times and then joined with a whole stitch. It is not until this point that the whole stitch with pairs is made. When the pairs leave the ground after the last whole stitch with pairs, thre is another whole stitch first, after which the pairs are twisted three times and re-enter the motifs or a ground.

Triangular ground

Figs. 57 and 58 show the prickings for the two directions of the Triangular ground. Fig. 59 is an illustration showing this ground with the apexes of the triangles to the right. Work this ground in whole stitch throughout. The diagram shows where and how many twists are required between the triangles. Fig. 59 also illustrates how this ground is joined to the footside and to a motif, and how many twists are required here.

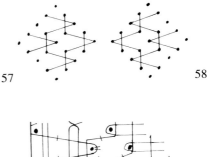

57   58

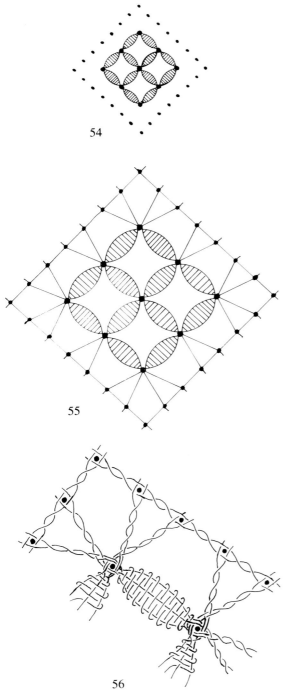

54

55

56

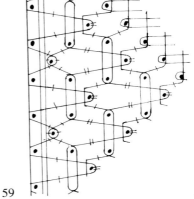

59

Plain Spiders

Fig. 60 shows the pricking for a spider. Fig. 61 is an illustration of this spider. You will notice that three pairs enter the spider from both sides. The number of twists depends on the number of pairs entering the spider from one side. Add one twist to this number. Subsequently the legs are twisted four times in the spider below. If there are four pairs, twist five times; if there are five pairs, twist six times, etc.

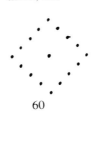

60

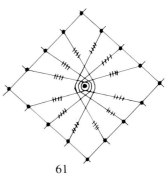

61

10

Tallies, diagonal and straight

Fig. 62 shows the pricking for two tallies in a Torchon ground. Fig. 63 illustrates the tallies and shows in which direction they are worked. In the diagram the lines in the tally indicate the direction of the worker thread.

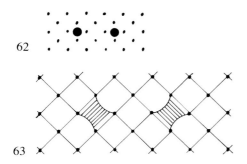

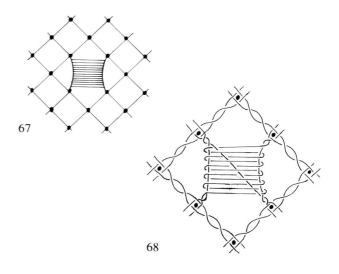

Figs. 64 and 65 show the course of the threads. Remember to twist the pairs twice before and after the tally.

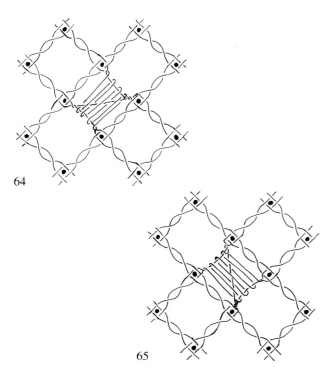

Fig. 66 shows the pricking for the straight tally, Fig. 67 is an illustration of the tally, and Fig. 68 shows the course of the threads of the straight tally. The instructions for the diagonal tally are also applied in the straight tally.

Flower with 6 petals

First the top three petals are worked. Work the heart in the following way:
Finish the middle petal with a half stitch, twist the pairs of the two other petals once. There are six pairs of bobbins for the heart. With the third pair whole stitch twice to the left, with the fourth pair whole stitch twice to the right; work a whole stitch with the pairs 2, 3, 4 and 5 (using them as single bobbins) and put in the pin. With the first pair whole stitch twice to the right, with the sixth pair whole stitch twice to the left. Now work the lower petals, starting the middle leaf with a whole stitch and the right and left leaf with a half stitch. See Fig. 69.

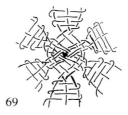

Flower with 8 petals

When the top four petals have been worked, all pairs are twisted once. Put in a pin at the end of each petal. Whole stitch the pairs in the heart (using them as if they were single bobbins). Put in a pin between the pairs and begin the three lower petals with a half stitch. See Fig. 70.

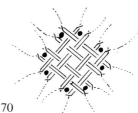

11

Half flowers along the footside

When the top two petals have been worked, the heart is worked as follows: consider the two pairs from the petal as a single pair and work a whole stitch with the worker pair from the footside. This is also done with the next petal. Put in a pin. Twist the worker pair twice and work back in the same way and make the footside. Start the lower petals with a half stitch again. See Fig. 71.

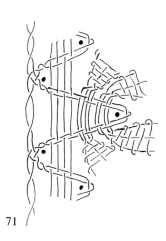

71

Motifs in whole stitch and half stitch

Fig. 72 shows the worker pair in a whole stitch zig-zag. Fig. 73 shows the same motif, but this time in half stitch. There are alternating workers in the half stitch zig-zag. Having put the pin at pinhole A, half stitch twice to the other side, put a pin at the next pinhole, twist the last passive pair once, and bring this pair to the other side as worker. See Fig. 73.

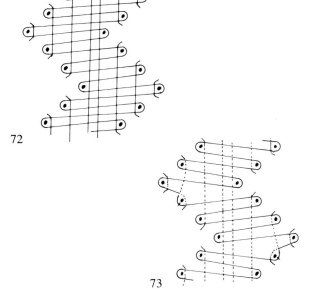

72

73

This method is used in all motifs in which a corner occurs and which are worked in half stitch.
Figs. 74 and 75 illustrate how motifs are split and joined and how many twists are required in the corner. Fig. 76 shows two diamonds passing into each other. At the middle pinhole the pairs are twisted once beside the pin.

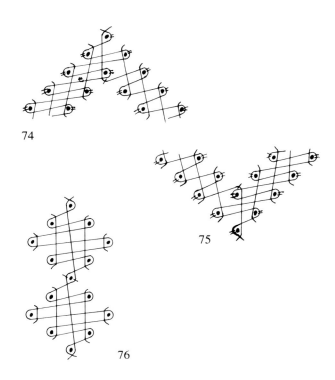

74

75

76

Passing gimps

Figs. 77 and 78 illustrate how gimps are passed: always over the lower and under the upper thread. Always twist the pairs twice before passing, no matter which stitch is used. Fig. 79 shows how two gimps pass each other.

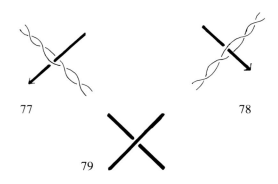

77

78

79

Toad's foot

In working a toad's foot there are several turns at the same pinhole in the corner.
Work whole stitch from the outer edge. The last stitch to be made is the turning stitch which is worked as follows: cross,

twist, twist and cross, put a pin between the second and third pair, work the second pair to the outer edge in whole stitch again. Now work inwards and make a turning stitch again with the last pair, take out the pin and replace it at the same pinhole between the second and third pair. Finish the toad's foot by replacing the pin again and again. When the toad's foot is finished the worker pair will be needed for other motifs, take out the pin before the last turning stitch and pull the worker pair carefully, otherwise there will be a loop at that place. See Fig. 80.

80

Heading of various fans

In the various fans the outer pair is always worked in whole stitch. This passive pair is always twisted twice to get a firm heading. See Fig. 81.

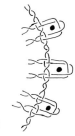

81

Tassels

Fig. 82 shows how the loops are joined in order to join a tassel to them.

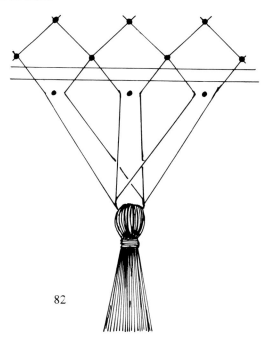

82

Sewing

If there are sewings in the middle of a lace, work to the middle pin, turn it round and twist five or six times. Twist the pair which is to be sewn, twice on your way back, and hook it to the other pair. Replace the pin so that it is in front of the sewn pair. Twist the pair which is to be sewn, twice, hook it to the other pair once more and twist twice again. Now continue working. See Fig. 83.

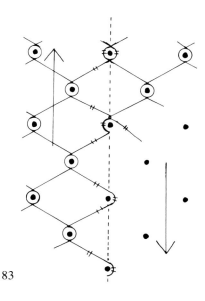

83

Some additional remarks

When turning round a pin the worker pair is always twisted twice.

The outer pairs of shells, waves and inwards waves are always worked whole stitch.

In a fan without a rib the traversing pairs are always twisted twice.

In a fan with a rib, the rib is always worked in whole stitches and the worker pair is twisted twice between the stitches.

The instructions for the plain spider, including those for the traversing pair, are also applied to the spider in the Spanish fan.

Twist the worker about ten times if you work a fringe, or loops for tassels.

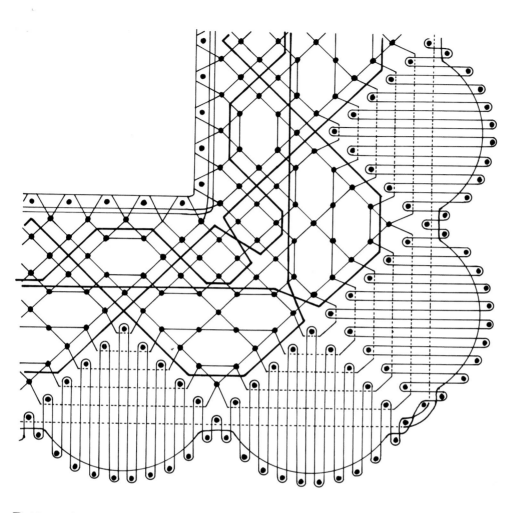

Pattern 1 17 pairs of bobbins, linen 40/2 and 4 bobbins,
linen 18/5

Pattern 2 17 pairs of bobbins, linen 90/2 and 4 bobbins,
linen 20/3

Pattern 3 17 pairs of bobbins, linen 90/2 and 4 bobbins,
linen 20/3

4

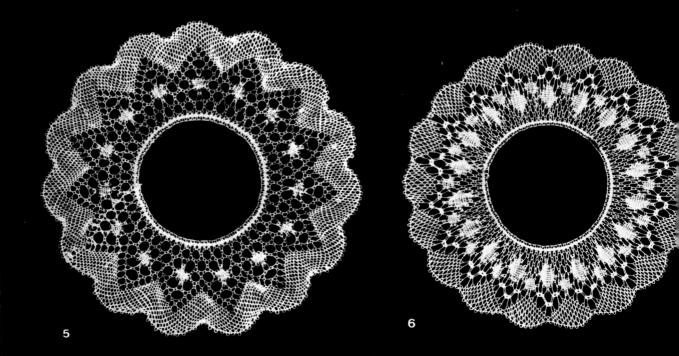

5   6

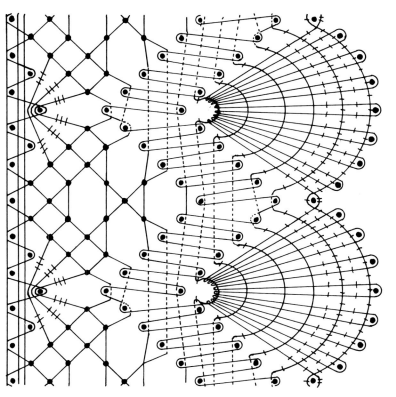

Pattern 4 20 pairs of bobbins, linen 60/2

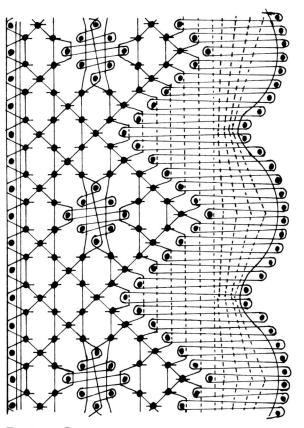

Pattern 5 23 pairs of bobbins, cotton 100/2

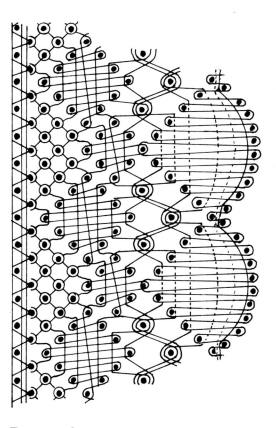

Pattern 6 20 pairs of bobbins, cotton 100/2

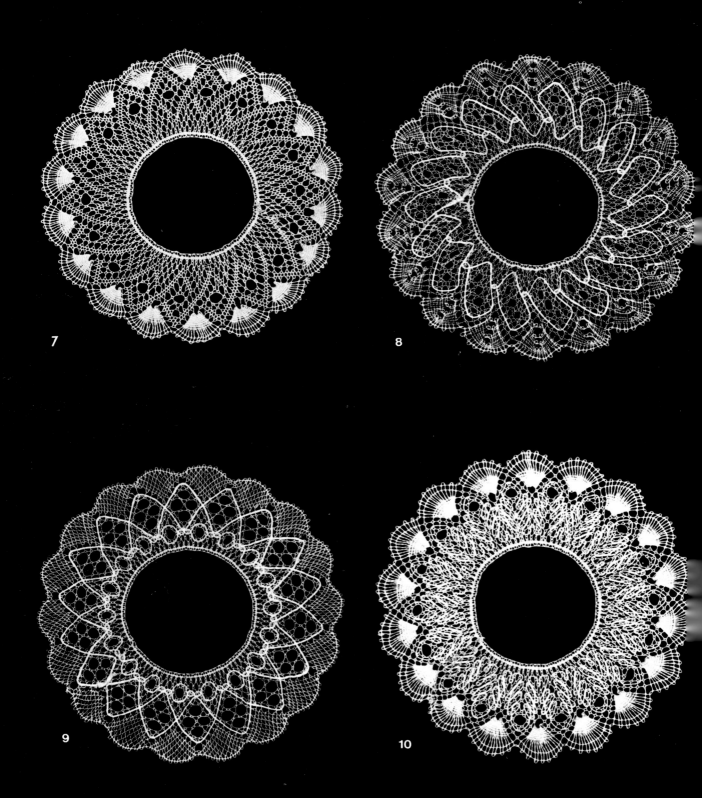

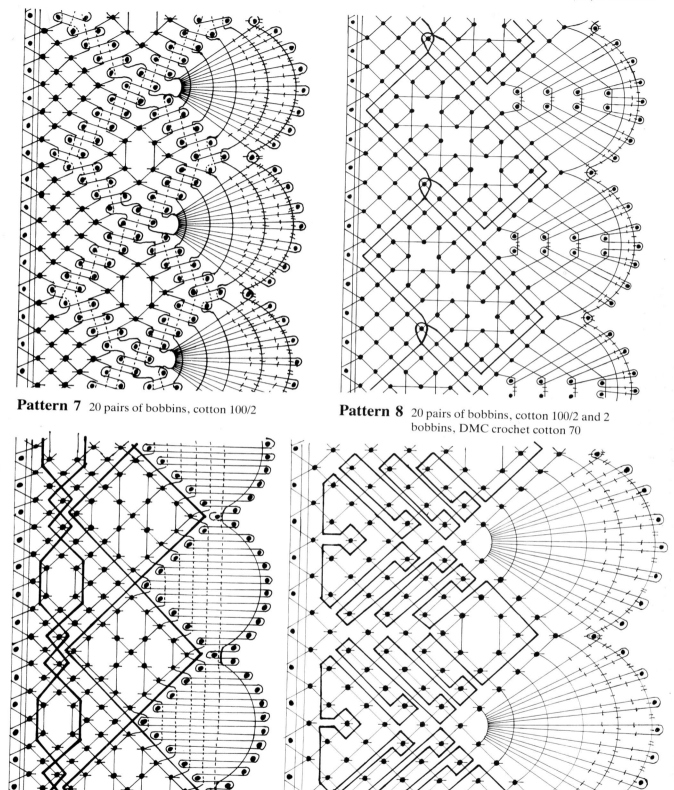

Pattern 7 20 pairs of bobbins, cotton 100/2

Pattern 8 20 pairs of bobbins, cotton 100/2 and 2 bobbins, DMC crochet cotton 70

Pattern 9 19 pairs of bobbins, cotton 100/2 and 4 bobbins, DMC crochet cotton 70

Pattern 10 20 pairs of bobbins, cotton 100/2 and 1 bobbin, DMC crochet cotton 70

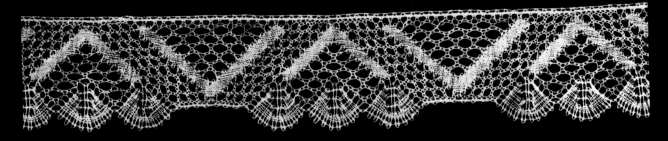

11

12

13

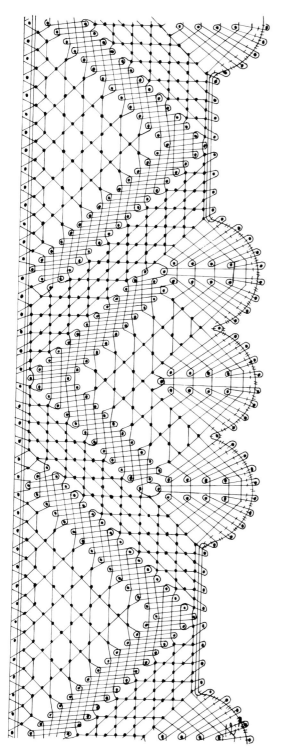

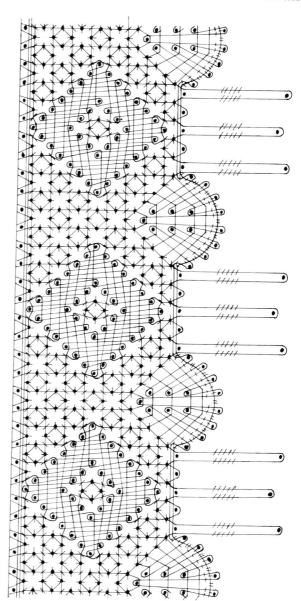

Pattern 12 22 pairs of bobbins, linen 100/2

Pattern 11 25 pairs of bobbins, linen 120/2

Pattern 13

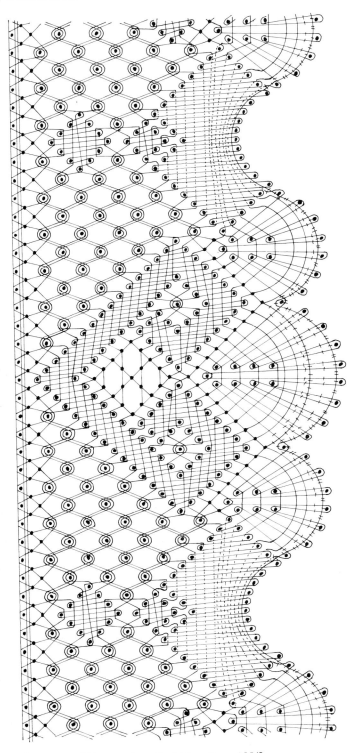

Pattern 13 32 pairs of bobbins, linen 100/2

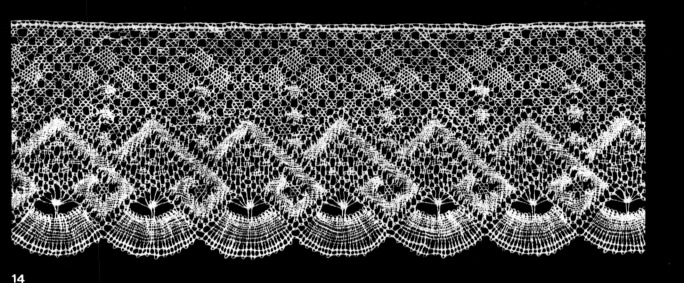

14

15

Patterns 14 and 15

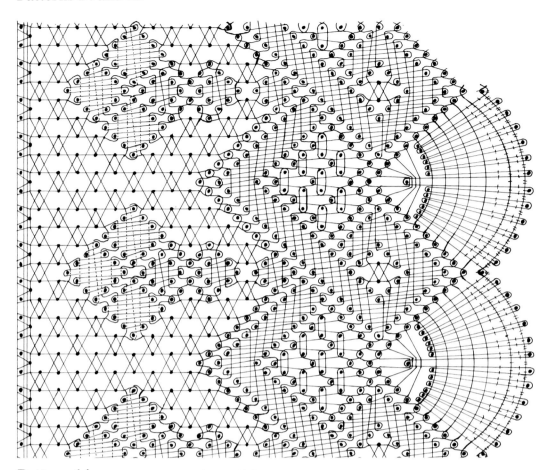

Pattern 14 53 pairs of bobbins, linen 120/2

Pattern 15 49 pairs of bobbins, linen 100/2

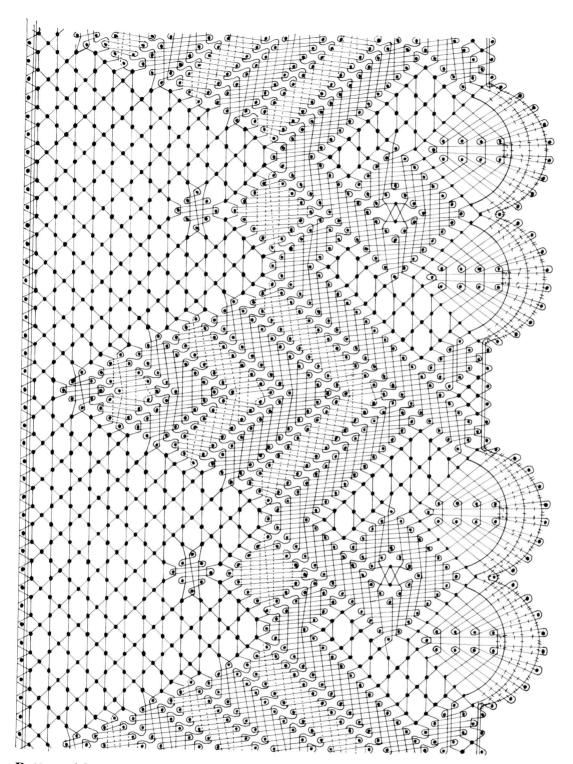

Pattern 16 54 pairs of bobbins, linen 100/2

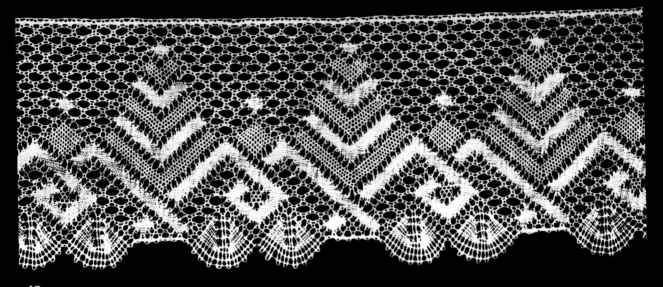

16

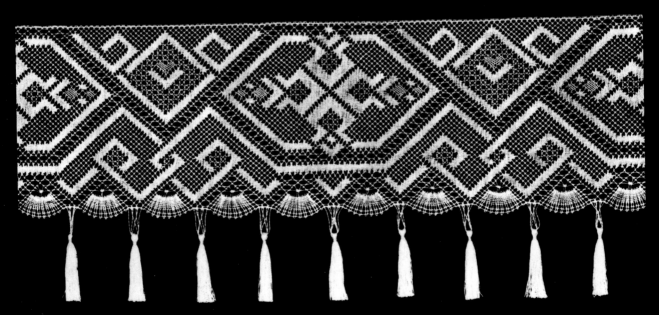

17

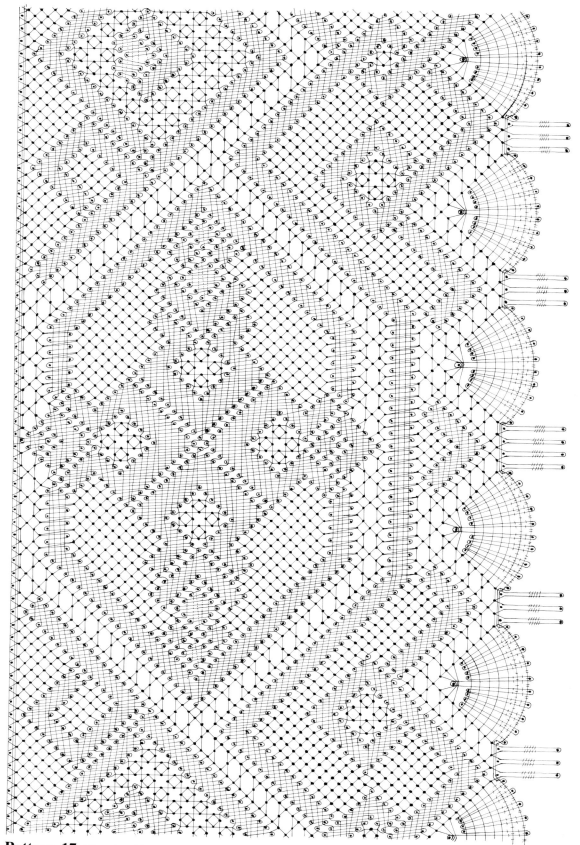

Pattern 17 79 pairs of bobbins, linen 50/2

For the sake of clarity this diagram has been drawn in
Torchon stitch, but the lace has been worked in Dieppe stitch.

18

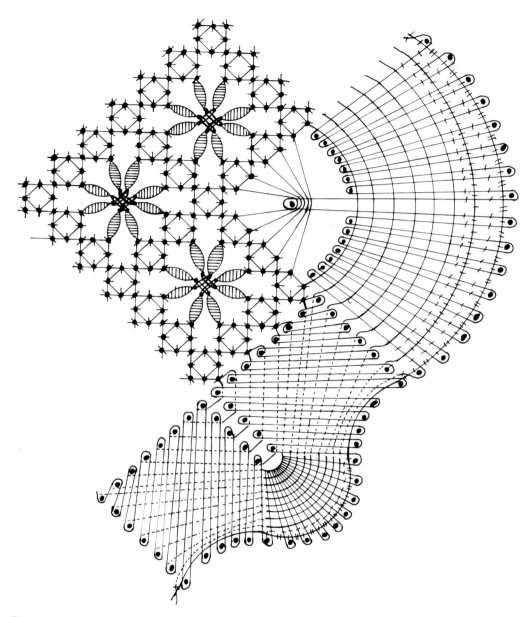

Pattern 18 30 pairs of bobbins, linen 50/2

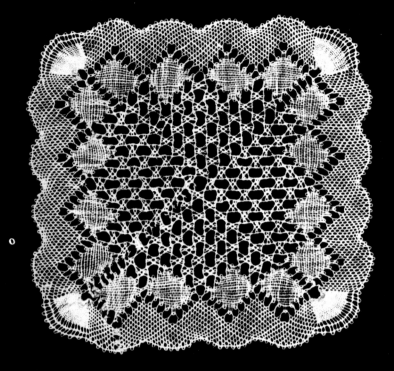

19

20

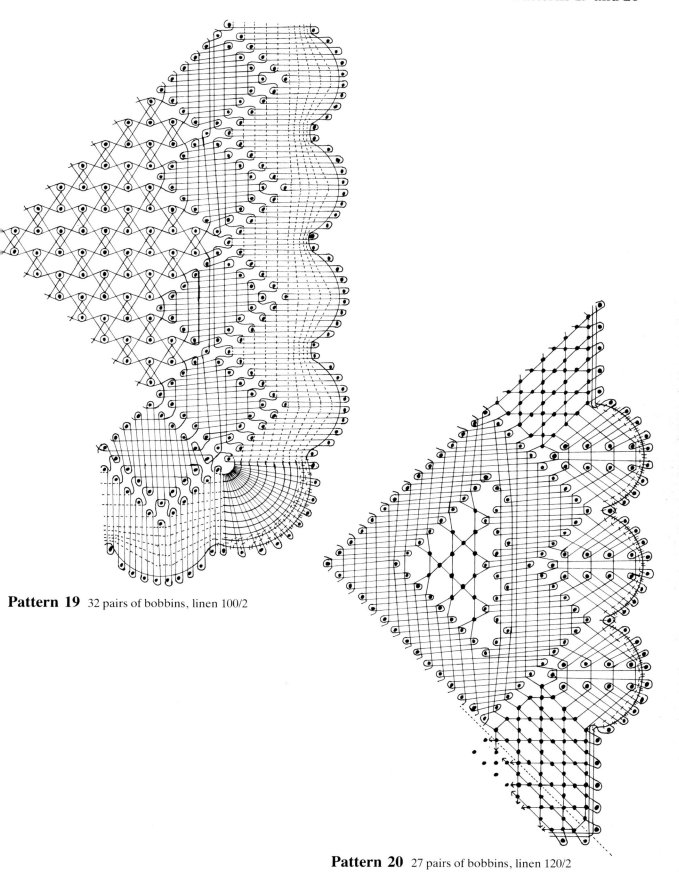

Pattern 19 32 pairs of bobbins, linen 100/2

Pattern 20 27 pairs of bobbins, linen 120/2

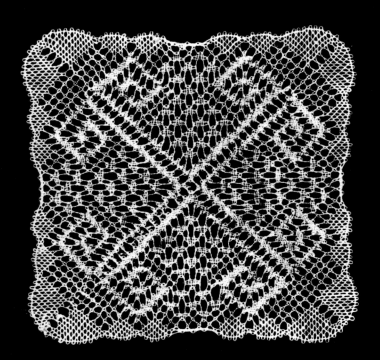

21

22

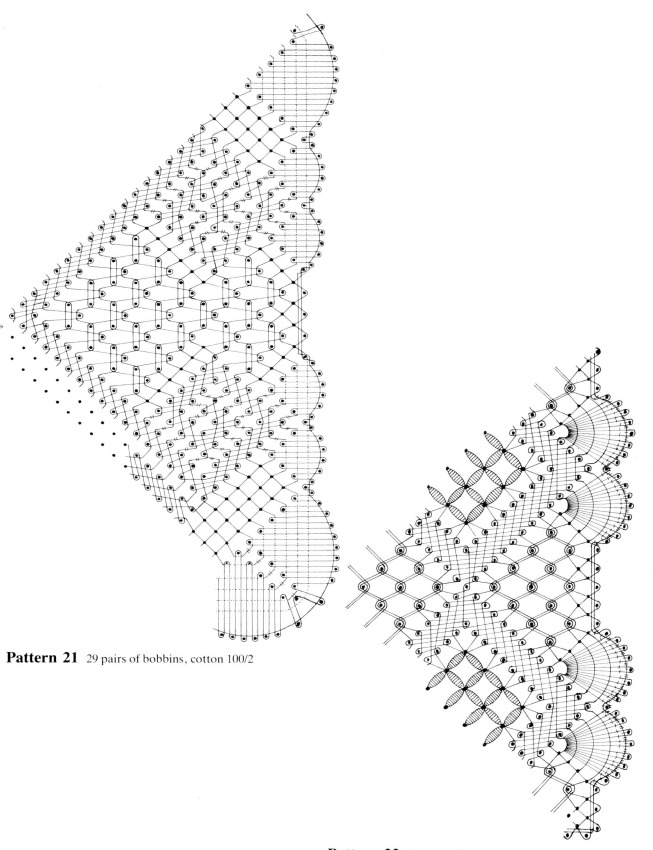

Pattern 21 29 pairs of bobbins, cotton 100/2

Pattern 22 29 pairs of bobbins, linen 120/2

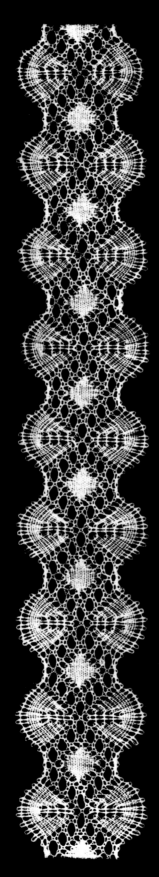

23

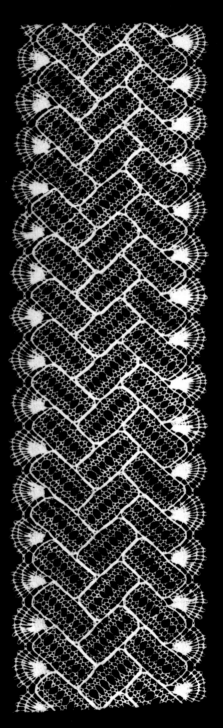

24

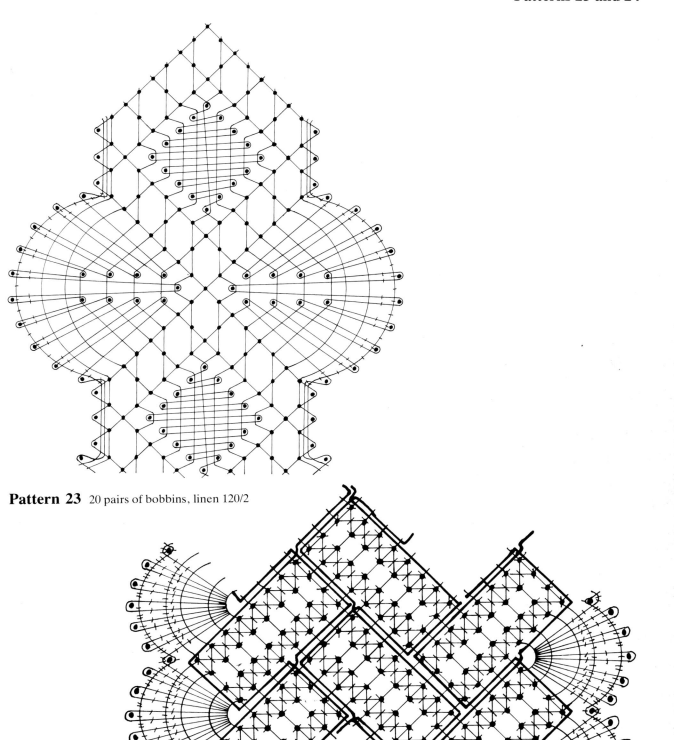

Pattern 23 20 pairs of bobbins, linen 120/2

Pattern 24 32 pairs of bobbins, linen 120/2 and 6 bobbins, linen 18/3

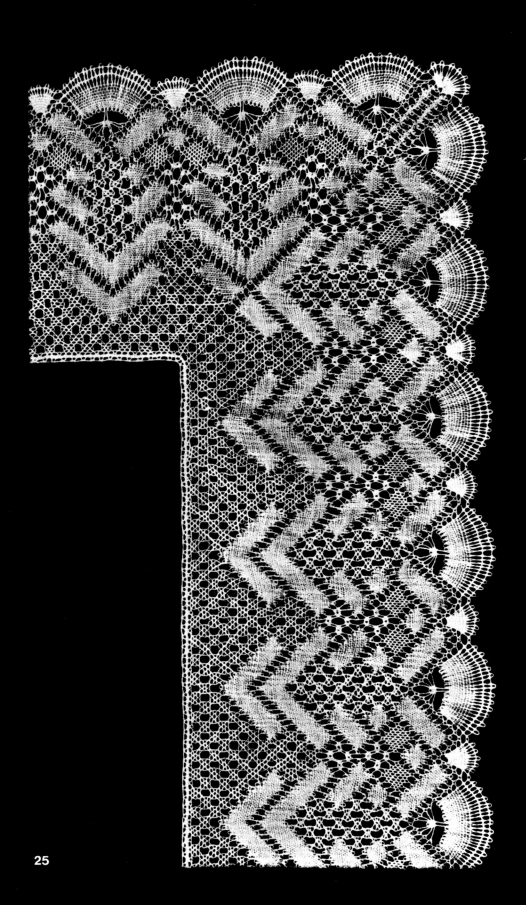

25

Pattern 25 63 pairs of bobbins, linen 100/2

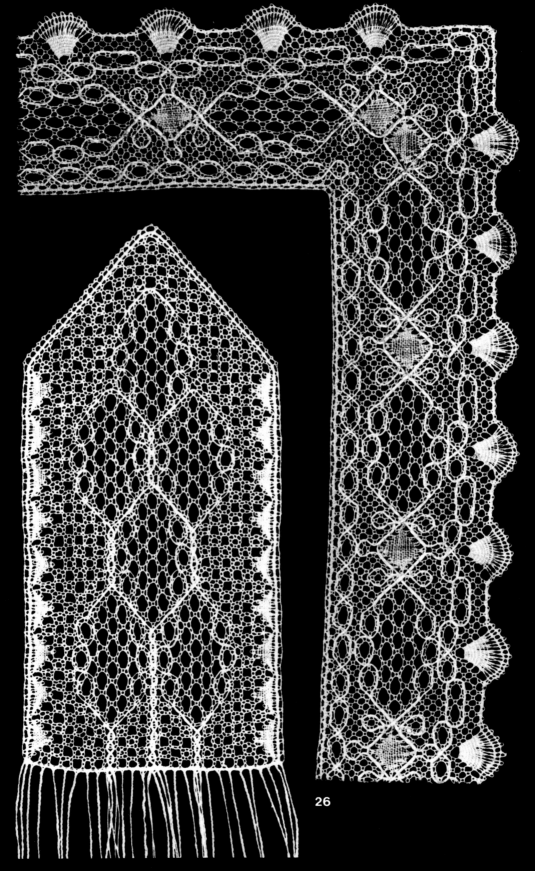

27   26

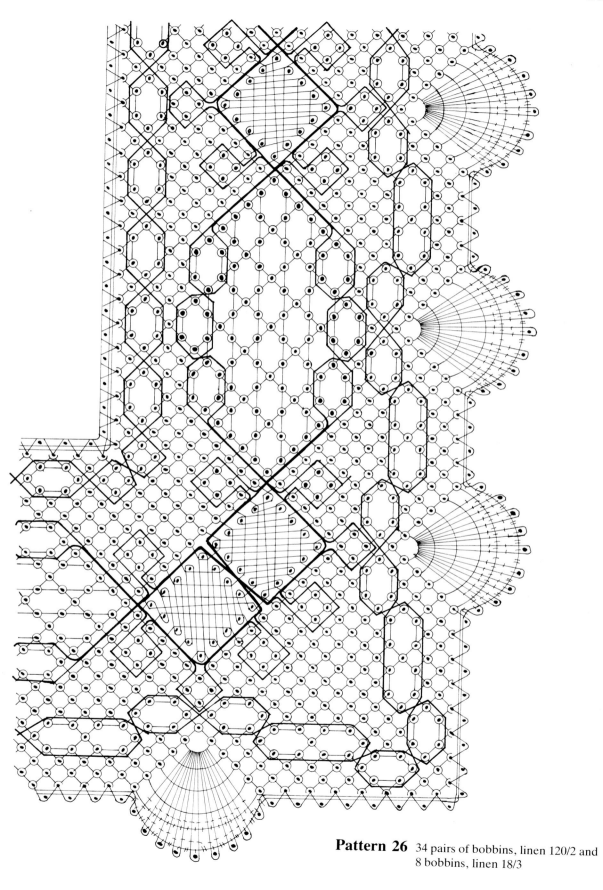

Pattern 26 34 pairs of bobbins, linen 120/2 and
8 bobbins, linen 18/3

Patterns 27 and 28

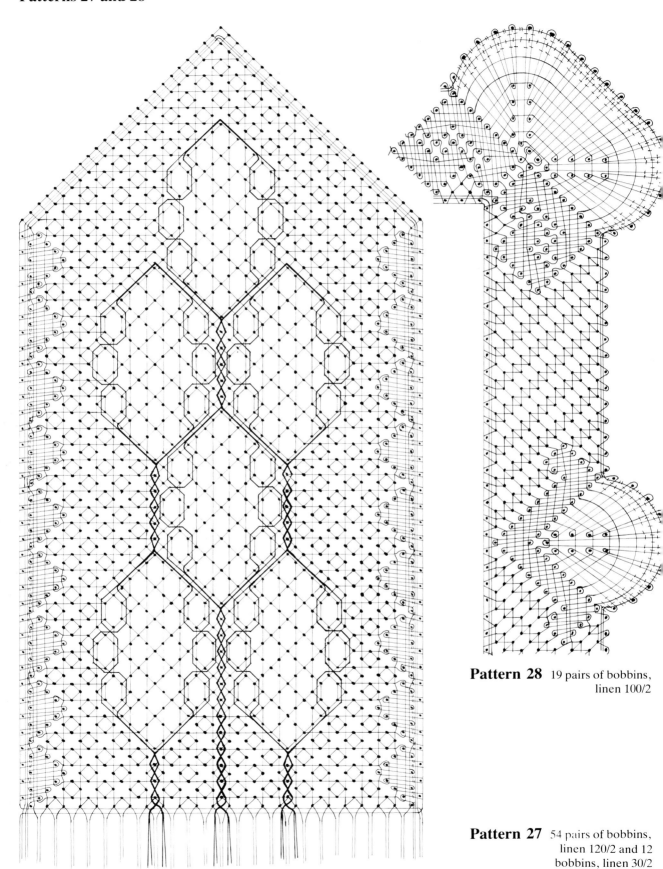

Pattern 28 19 pairs of bobbins, linen 100/2

Pattern 27 54 pairs of bobbins, linen 120/2 and 12 bobbins, linen 30/2

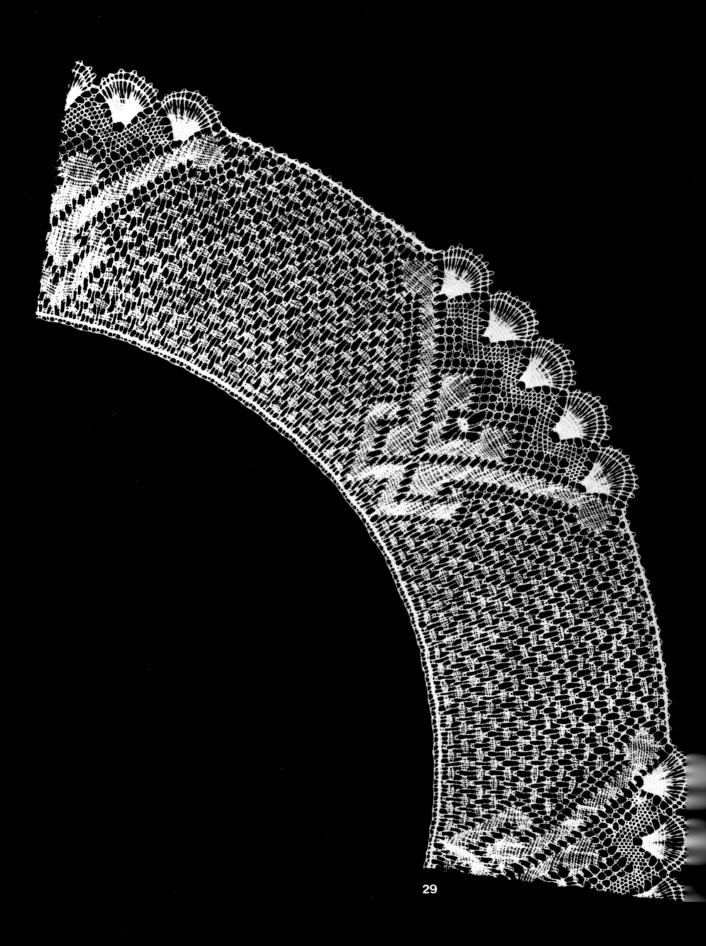

29

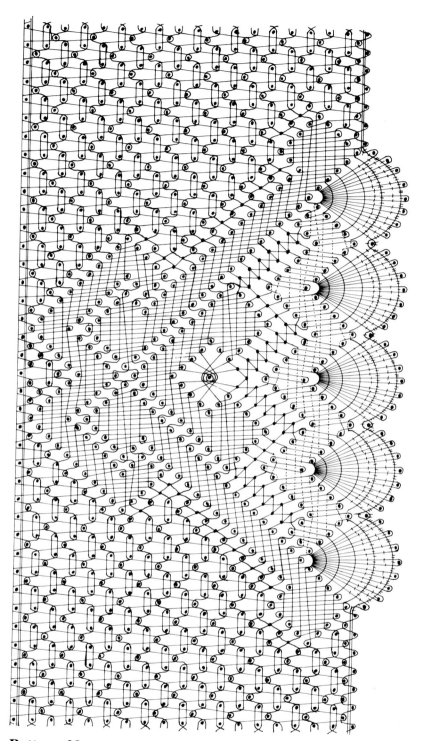

Pattern 29 41 pairs of bobbins, linen 100/2

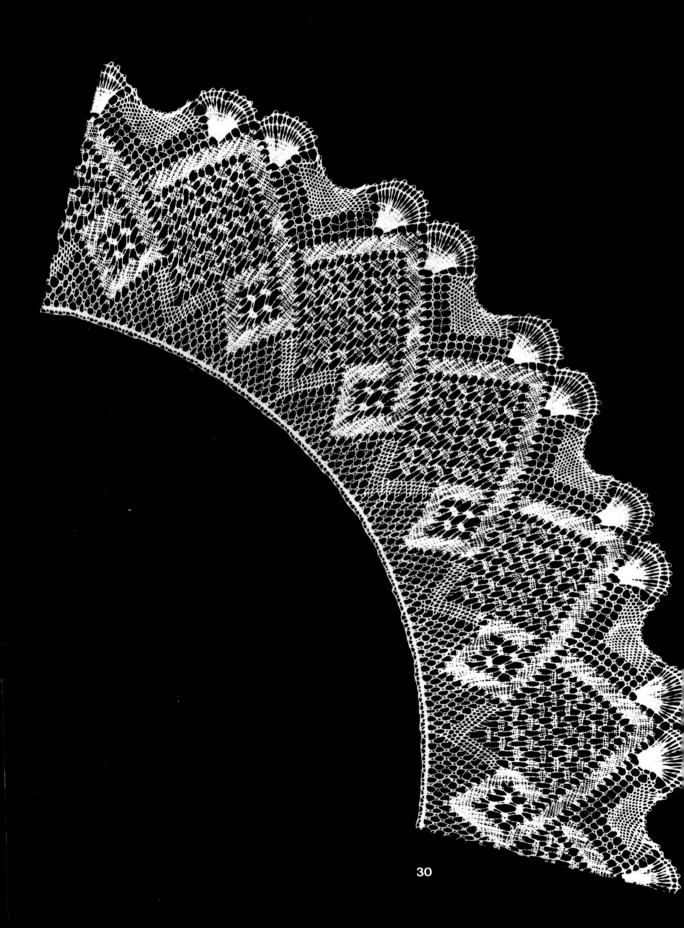

30

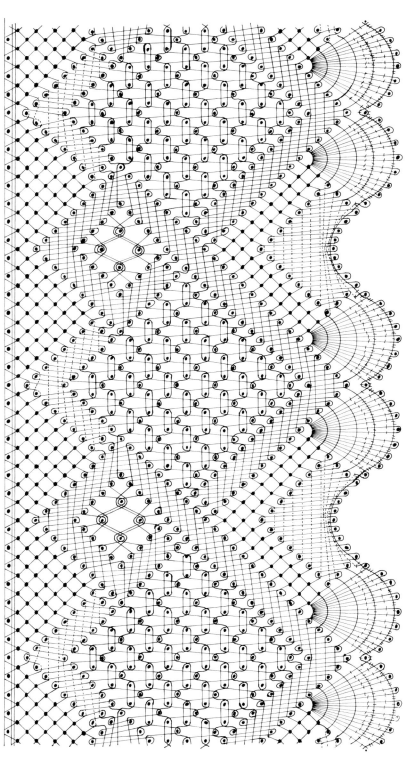

Pattern 30 42 pairs of bobbins, linen 100/2

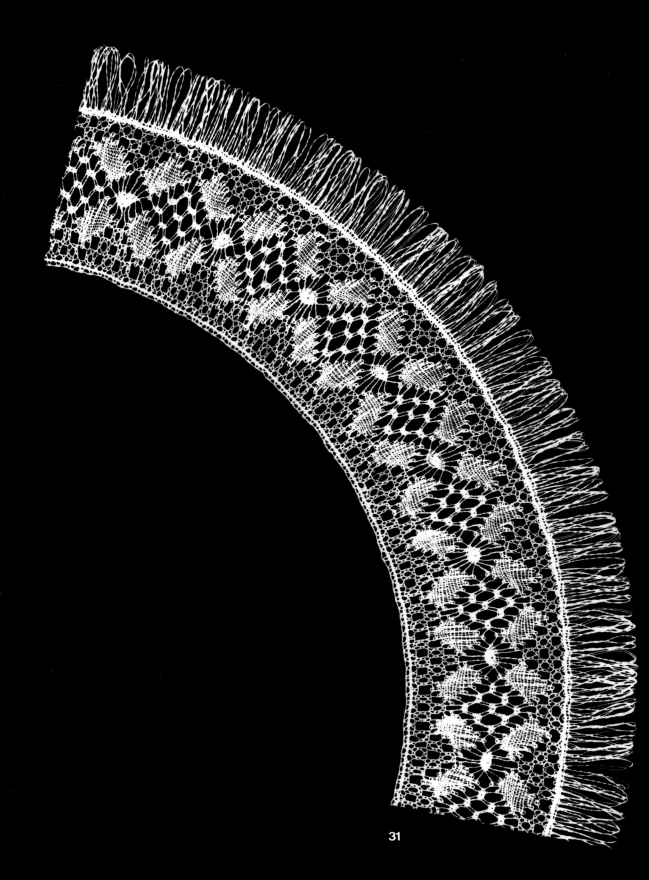

31

Pattern 31 30 pairs of bobbins, linen 120/2

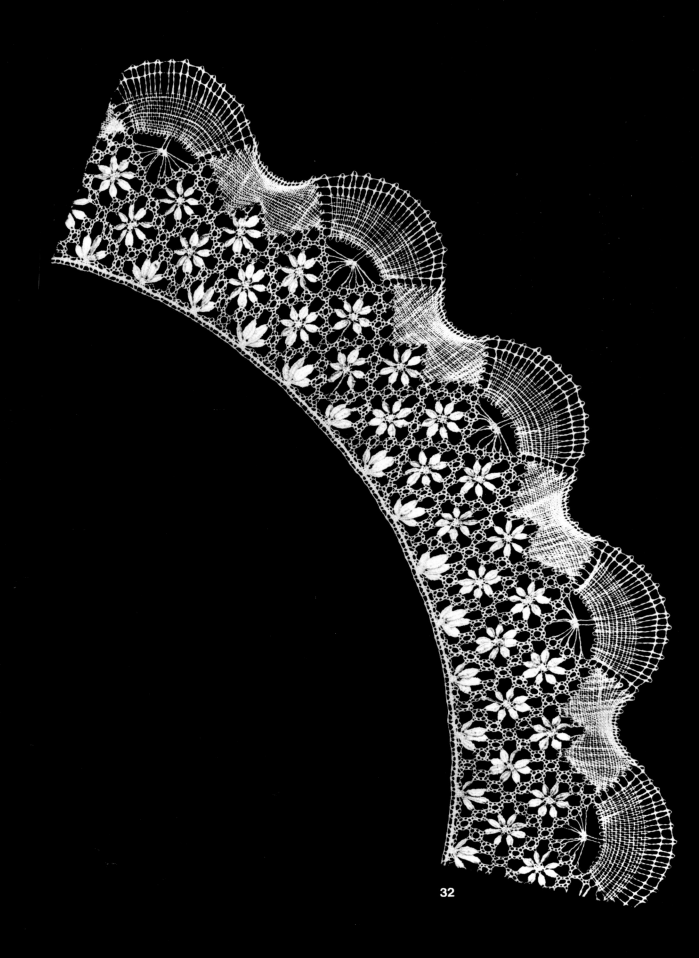

32

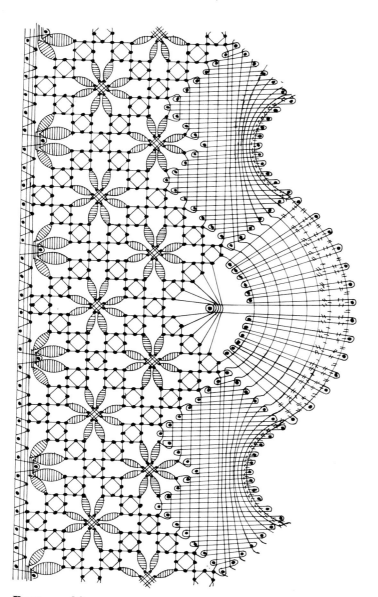

Pattern 32 33 pairs of bobbins, linen 100/2

33

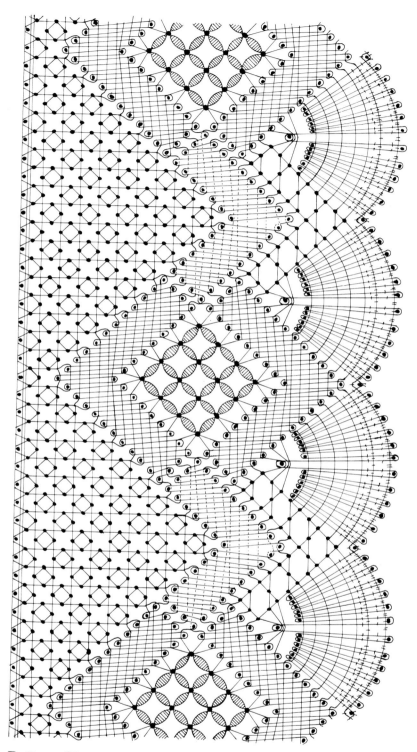

Pattern 33 40 pairs of bobbins, linen 100/2

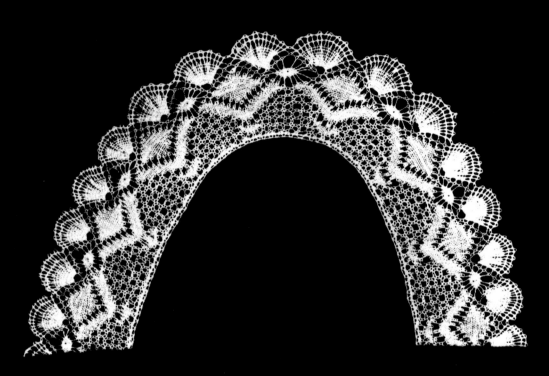

34

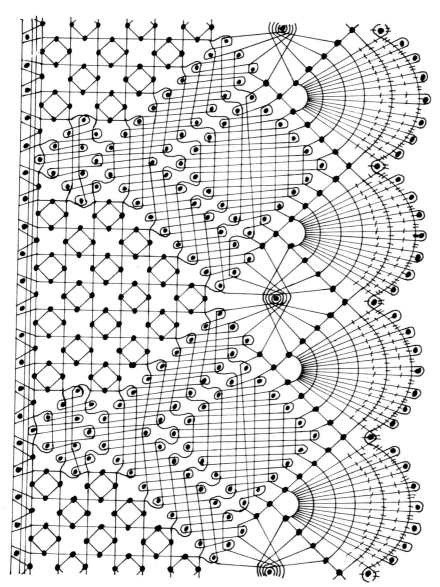

Pattern 34 29 pairs of bobbins, linen 120/2

35

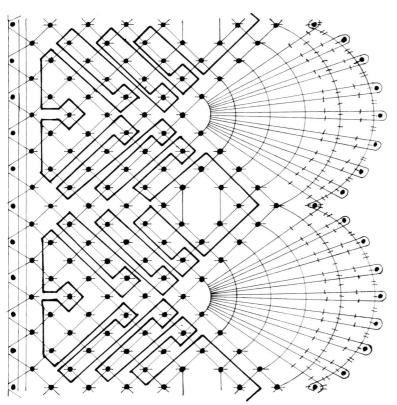

Pattern 35 20 pairs of bobbins, linen 140/2 and 1
bobbin, linen 40/2

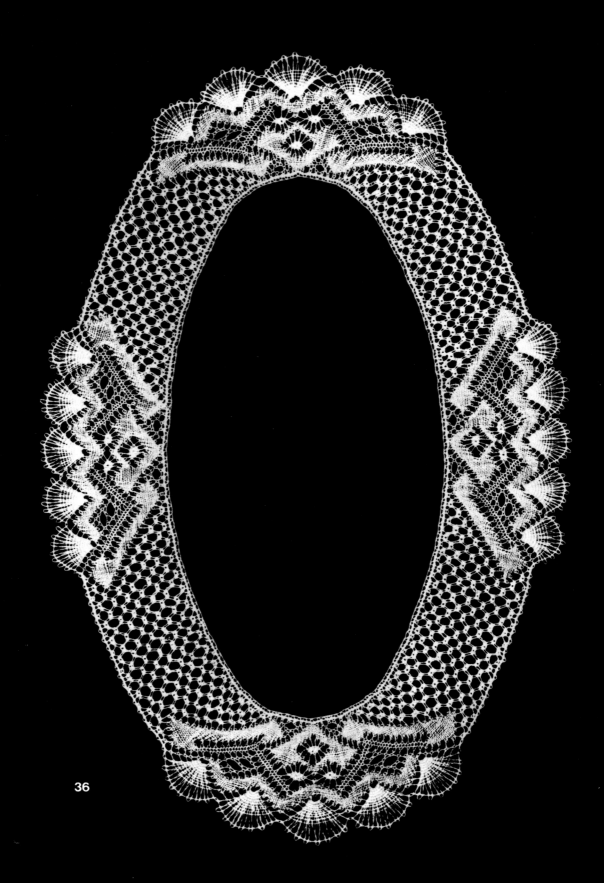

36

Pattern 36 31 pairs of bobbins, linen 140/2

37

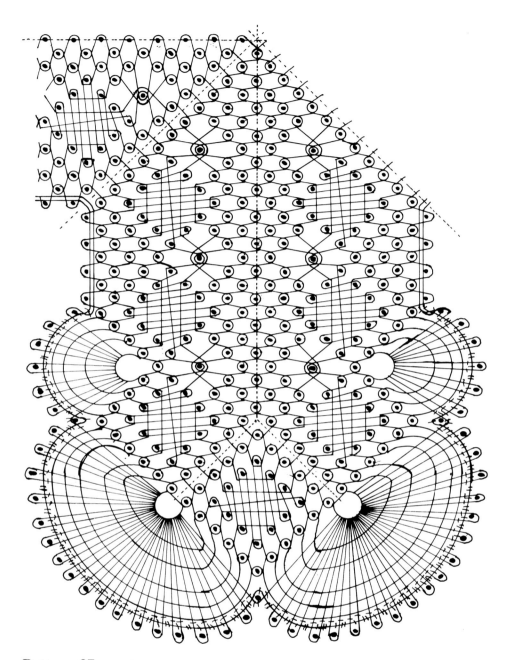

Pattern 37 14 pairs of bobbins, linen 100/2

38

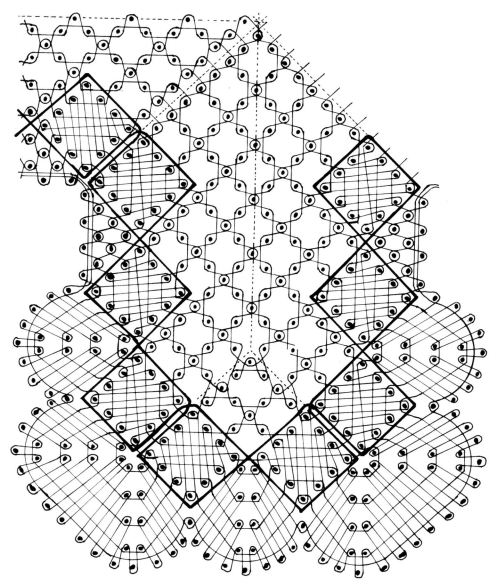

Pattern 38 14 pairs of bobbins, linen 120/2 and 2
bobbins, linen 18/3

39

Pattern 39 87 pairs of bobbins, linen 120/2

Pattern 40 62 pairs of bobbins, linen 60/2
If — after setting up — you start working on the right-hand side of the lace, and work from the left to the right as much as possible, it is possible to work the whole pattern with the same number of bobbins.

The lace on the photograph has been worked in Dieppe stitch.
There is no working diagram for this pattern; refer to the pricking for the working method.

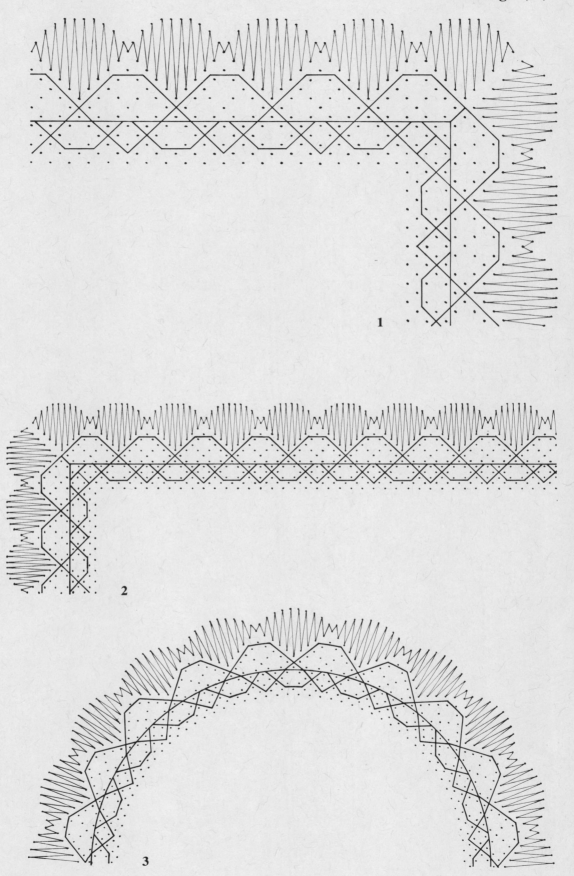

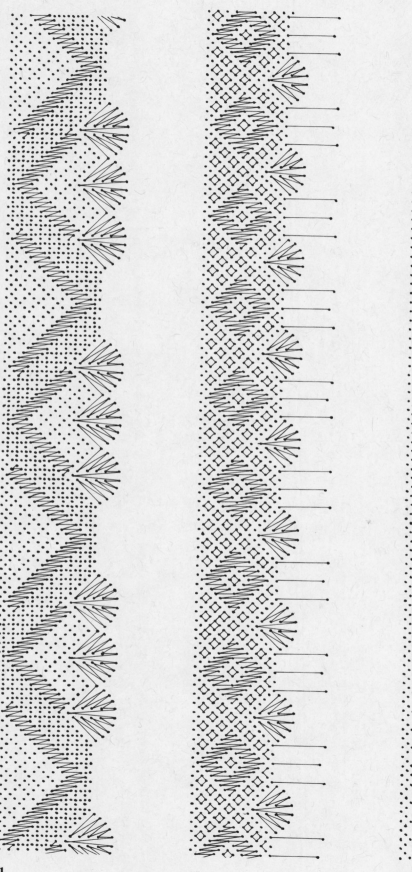
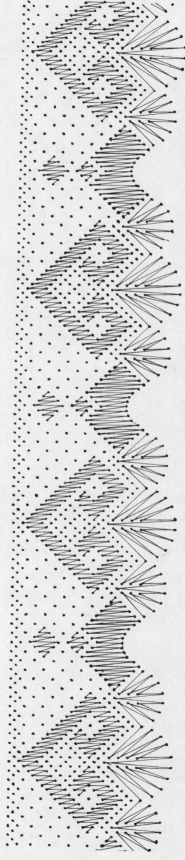

11

12

13

14

15

17a

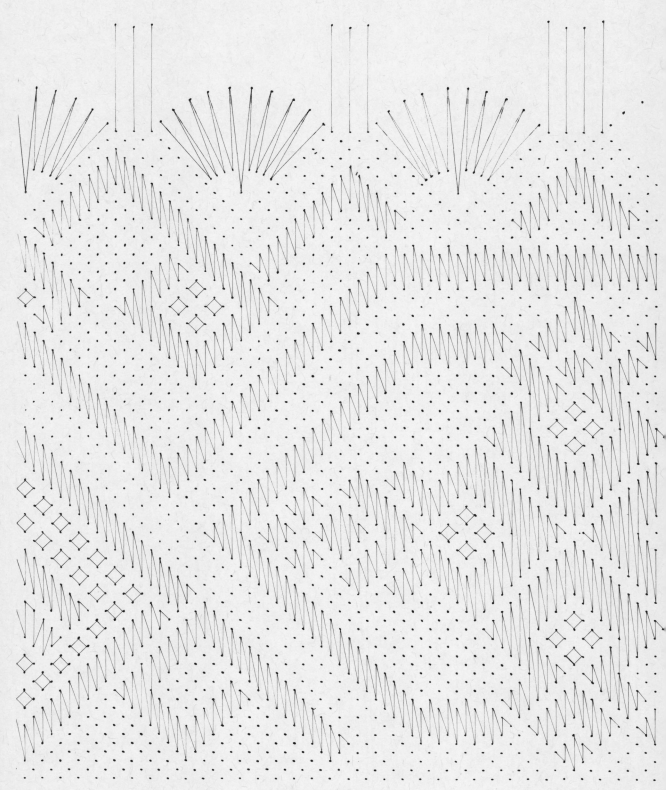

17b

19

20

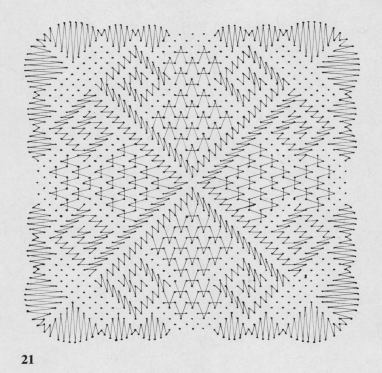

21

22

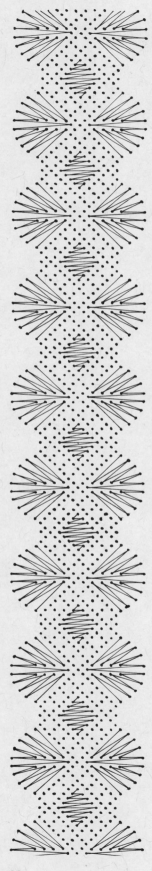

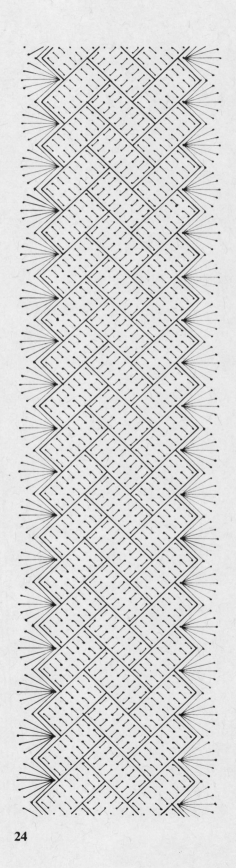

23

24

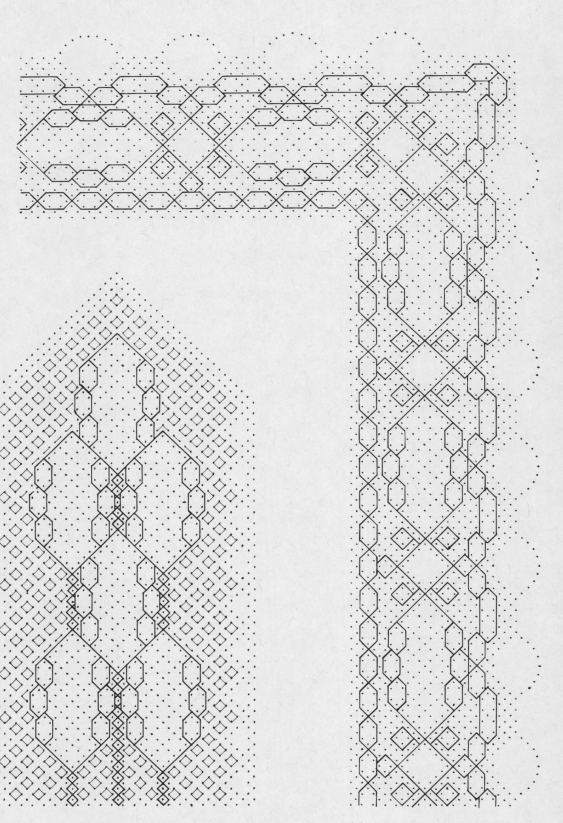

28

Pricking 29

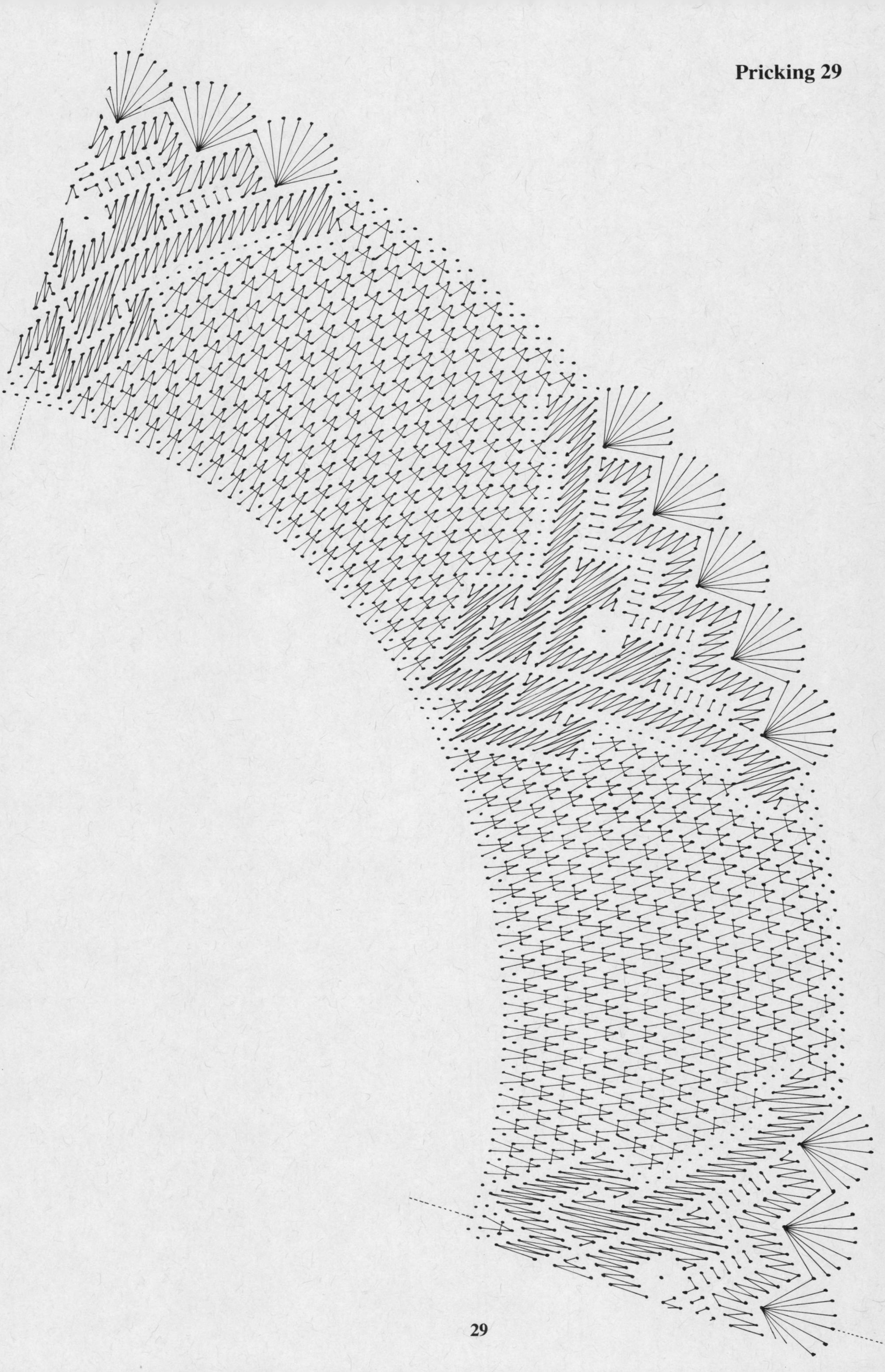

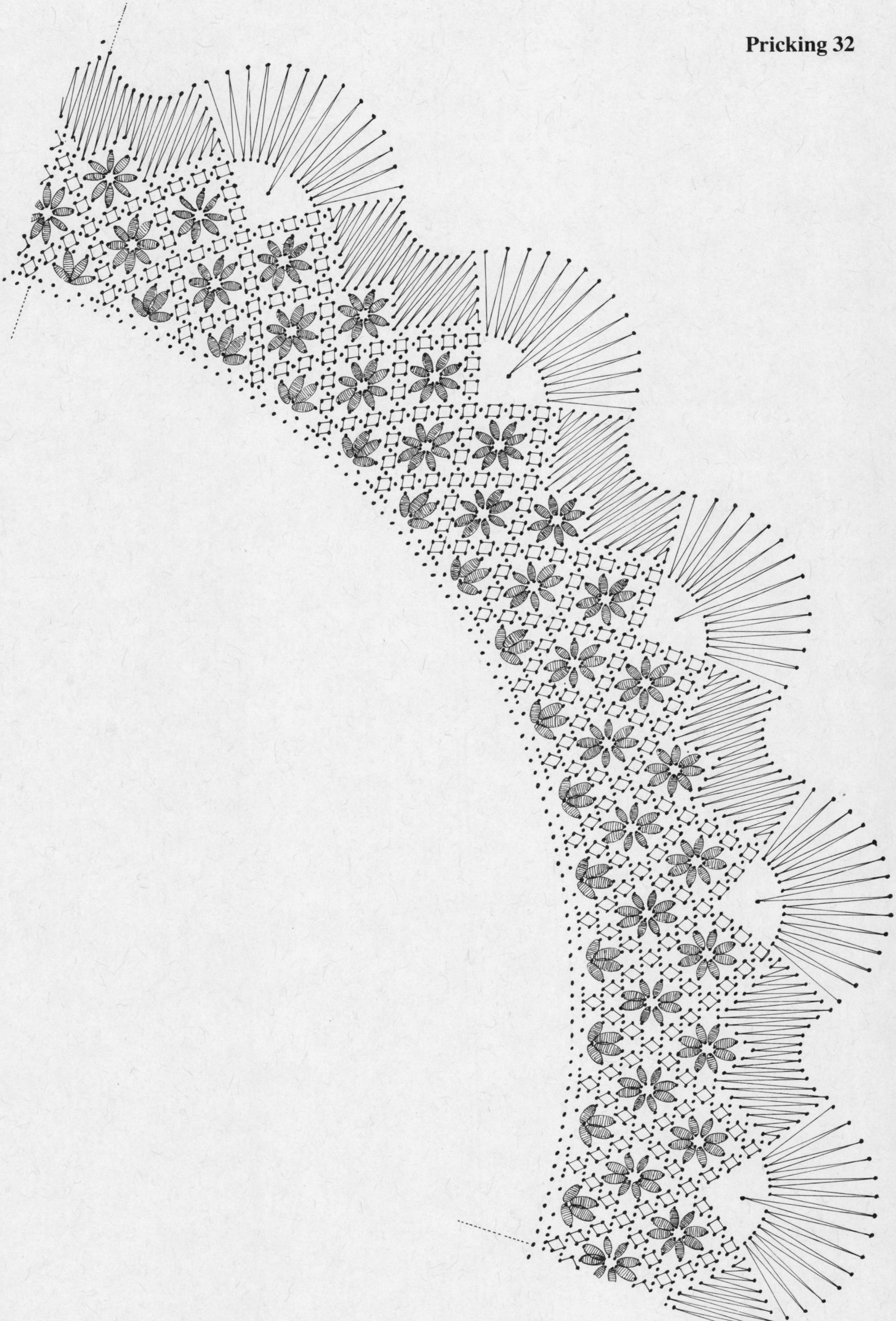

Pricking 33

37

38

39a

39b

39c

39d

39e

39f

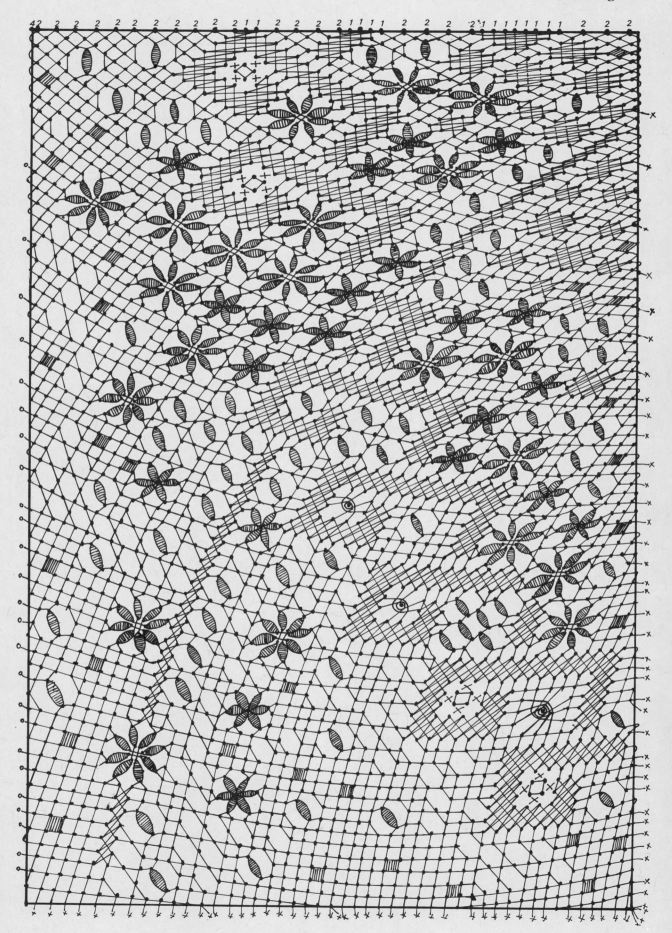